19 ROSWELL BRANCH

D0931304

19 ROSKILL RN.

A Kid's Guide to Drawing America™

How to Draw
New Mexico's
Sights and Symbols

Aileen Weintraub

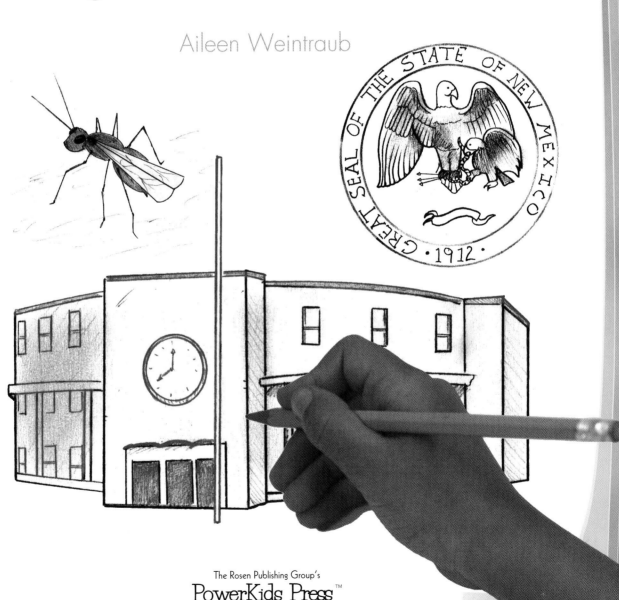

19 ROSWELL BRANCH

The Rosen Publishing Group's
PowerKids Press™
New York

Published in 2002 by The Rosen Publishing Group, Inc.
29 East 21st Street, New York, NY 10010

Copyright © 2002 by The Rosen Publishing Group, Inc.

All rights reserved. No part of this book may be reproduced in any form without permission in writing from the publisher, except by a reviewer.

First Edition

Project Editor: Jennifer Landau
Book Design: Kim Sonsky
Layout Design: Nick Scaccia

Illustration Credits: Jamie Grecco
Photo Credits: p. 7 © Joseph Sohm; ChromoSohm Inc./CORBIS; p. 8 © Joe Munroe/Hulton Archive by Getty Images; p. 9 © Milwaukee Art Museum, Gift of Jane B. Pettit Foundation and The Georgia O'Keeffe Foundation; pp. 12, 14 © One Mile Up, Incorporated; p. 16 © David Muench/CORBIS; p. 18 © Steve Kaufman/CORBIS; p. 20 © Buddy Mays/CORBIS; p. 22 © Index Stock; p. 24 © Martin McKenna; p. 26 © Gary W. Carter/CORBIS; p. 28 © Liz Hymans/CORBIS.

Weintraub, Aileen, 1973–
        How to draw New Mexico's sights and symbols /
Aileen Weintraub.
                p. cm. — (A kid's guide to drawing America)
        Includes index.
        Summary: This book explains how to draw some of New Mexico's sights and symbols, including the state seal and the official flower.
        ISBN 0-8239-6087-0
        1. Emblems, State—New Mexico—Juvenile literature 2. New Mexico—In art—Juvenile literature   3. Drawing—Technique—Juvenile literature   [1. Emblems, State—New Mexico 2. New Mexico   3. Drawing—Technique]
I. Title   II. Series
                2002
        743'.8'99789—dc21

Manufactured in the United States of America

CONTENTS

Let's Draw New Mexico

Native Americans began settling the land we now call New Mexico in prehistoric times. Since then New Mexico has been part of Spain, Mexico, and the United States. In 1540, Spanish explorer Juan Vásquez de Coronado arrived in this land while searching for the mythical Seven Cities of Cibola. These cities were supposed to be filled with gold. Coronado did not find these cities. Instead he found Native American villages called pueblos. The Spaniards took over the land and tried to convert the Native Americans to Christianity.

Spain also ruled the country of Mexico from the 1500s to the 1800s. In 1821, Mexico won independence from Spain. Mexico took control of New Mexico and opened trade with the United States. The Mexican War, fought between Mexico and the United States, began in 1846. This war decided the ownership of New Mexico. When the war ended in 1848, the territory of New Mexico became part of the United States. New Mexico became the forty-seventh state on January 6, 1912.

New Mexico is known for its many natural wonders,

including Carlsbad Caverns. These caverns make up the third-longest cave system in the world. Another natural wonder is the White Sands National Monument. It is famous for its sand dunes and is one of the world's largest deposits of gypsum.

With the help of this book, you will learn how to draw some of New Mexico's sights and symbols. The drawings start with simple shapes. New steps are shown in red. Directions under each step will help guide you.

The supplies you will need to draw New Mexico's sights and symbols are:

- A sketch pad
- An eraser
- A number 2 pencil
- A pencil sharpener

These are some of the shapes and drawing terms you need to know to draw New Mexico's sights and symbols:

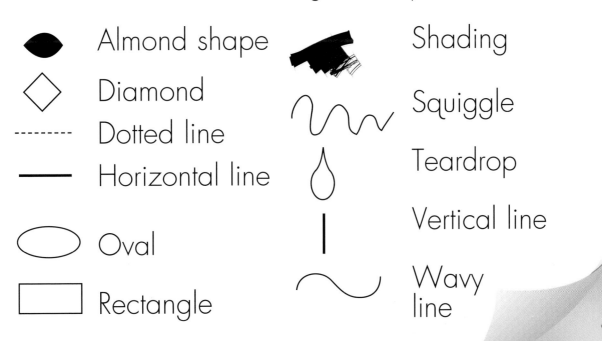

Almond shape

Diamond

Dotted line

Horizontal line

Oval

Rectangle

Shading

Squiggle

Teardrop

Vertical line

Wavy line

The Land of Enchantment

New Mexico is a state with many cultures. It has Native American, Spanish, and North American influences. This background contributes to the state's beautiful adobe architecture, to its clothing styles, and even to its yearly festivals. Spanish settlers brought chile peppers to New Mexico. The chile pepper has since become the state vegetable. There are now chile festivals to see who can grow the hottest peppers. Every year there is also a hot-air balloon festival in Albuquerque, New Mexico's most populated city. New Mexico's nickname is the Land of Enchantment. The state certainly has much to offer residents and visitors.

In the 1870s, gold mining was a big industry in the United States. Many people traveled the Santa Fe Trail, which cuts through New Mexico, in search of their fortune. The city of Santa Fe has been the capital of New Mexico since 1610. Today major industries in New Mexico include agriculture, mining, and tourism.

Hot-air balloons take flight during the Albuquerque International Balloon Fiesta in Albuquerque, New Mexico.

Artist in New Mexico

Georgia O'Keeffe

Artist Georgia O'Keeffe was inspired by New Mexico's landscape. She created much artwork from what she saw and experienced in this state. O'Keeffe was born on November 15, 1887, in Sun Prairie, Wisconsin. She loved art and took drawing lessons as a child. By eighth grade, she knew she wanted to be a professional artist. She studied art in Chicago and in New York. In 1924, she married a famous photographer named Alfred Stieglitz. He encouraged O'Keeffe's career as a painter.

Starting in 1929, O'Keeffe spent her summers painting in New Mexico. She displayed her work at galleries and at exhibitions. O'Keeffe painted close-up pictures of objects, like flowers, using bold brush strokes and sharp lines. O'Keeffe also was known for painting pictures of animal skulls and New Mexico scenery. After O'Keeffe's husband died, she moved to

New Mexico permanently. She continued painting until the late 1970s, when her eyesight failed. At this point, O'Keeffe stopped painting and started making clay sculptures. O'Keeffe lived to be 98 years old. She died in 1986. In 1997, the Georgia O'Keeffe Museum opened in Santa Fe, New Mexico, to honor the work of this great artist.

© Milwaukee Art Museum, Gift of Jane B. Pettit Foundation and the Georgia O'Keefe Foundation

In 1938, Georgia O'Keeffe painted *The Cliff Chimneys* in oil on canvas, which measures 36" x 30" (91 cm x 76 cm). O'Keeffe often painted scenes from the area surrounding her New Mexico home.

Map of New Mexico

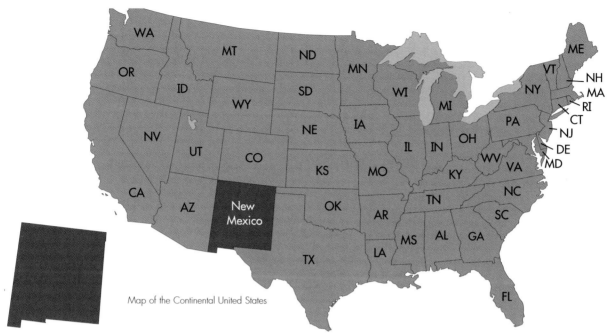

Map of the Continental United States

New Mexico has some of the best weather in the United States. The state has high mountains and flat deserts, allowing for warm days and cool nights. New Mexico is one of the four-corner states. This means that it borders three other states at the same point. These other three states are Colorado, Utah, and Arizona. New Mexico also shares an international border with Mexico. The highest point in the state is Wheeler Peak at 13,161 feet (4,011 m) high. New Mexico is the fifth-largest state in the country. It is 121,599 square miles (314,940 sq km). The beautiful Rio Grande runs through the state. Rio Grande means "big river" in Spanish. Most New Mexicans live along this river.

1

Start by drawing a slanted rectangle.

2

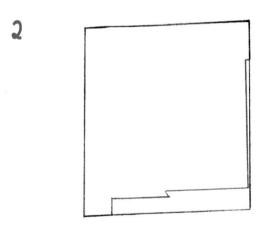

Using the rectangle as a guide, draw the shape of New Mexico.

3

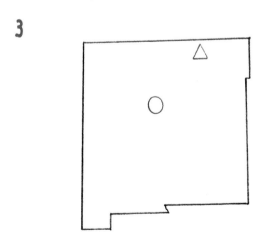

Erase extra lines and draw a triangle for Wheeler Peak and a circle for Albuquerque.

4

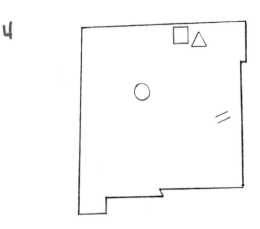

Draw a square to mark Carson National Forest and draw two slanted lines for Conchas Dam.

5

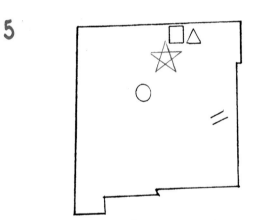

Draw a star to mark Santa Fe, the capital of New Mexico.

6

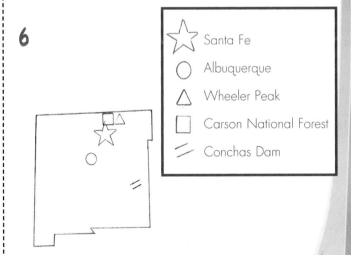

☆	Santa Fe
○	Albuquerque
△	Wheeler Peak
□	Carson National Forest
⁄⁄	Conchas Dam

Erase extra lines in the star. Draw a key in the upper right corner to mark these New Mexican points of interest.

The State Seal

The first seal of New Mexico was designed in 1851. In 1913, the final touches were put on a new seal that had begun to take shape in the late 1860s. It shows an American bald eagle protecting a smaller Mexican eagle with its wings. This represents the change in government from Mexico to the United States. The American bald eagle represents bravery and strength. It is holding three arrows in its talons. The Mexican eagle has a snake in its beak and a cactus in its talons. This is taken from an Aztec myth that says the Aztec people should settle in the place where they see an eagle about to eat a snake. Written on the scroll beneath the eagle is "*Crescit Eundo*". This is New Mexico's state motto and is Latin for "it grows as it goes."

1

Start by drawing two large circles. Add five small circles for the shape of the large eagle.

2

Draw the outline of the eagle. For the legs, draw two slanted vertical lines, a line connecting them, and a line up the middle.

3

Add detail to the large eagle. Erase extra lines. Add three circles for the small eagle.

4

Draw the shape of the small eagle using the circles as guides.

5

Erase extra lines. Add arrows in the large eagle's talons and a snake in the small eagle's mouth. Add a small rectangle for the banner.

6

Add the words "GREAT SEAL OF THE STATE OF NEW MEXICO" and the year 1912. Add detail and shading.

13

The State Flag

Ralph Emerson Twitchell, a historian of New Mexico, designed the first state flag in 1915. It had a blue field with a U.S. flag in the upper left corner and the state seal in the lower right corner. In 1925, Santa Fe resident Dr. Harry Mera won a contest for the New Mexico state flag by using a design made by his wife Reba. Dr. Mera chose a red Zia on a field of gold. The Zia, New Mexico's state emblem, is an ancient Native American sun symbol that looks like a circle with four points. Each point is made of four lines. In the Native American culture, four is a sacred number. This number represents the earth, the year, the day, and life. Red and gold represent the time of Spanish rule, which lasted from 1598 to 1821.

1

Start by drawing a large rectangle for the flag's field.

2

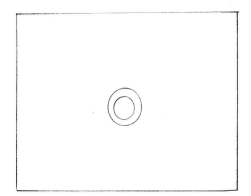

Add two circles in the center.

3

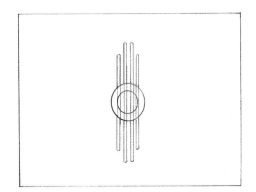

Draw four thin, tubelike shapes as shown.

4

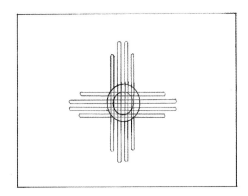

Draw four more tubelike shapes horizontally.

5

Erase extra lines and smudges.

6

Shade or color your flag, and you're done.

The Yucca

A group of schoolchildren in New Mexico took a vote to decide what the state flower should be. This is how, on March 14, 1927, the yucca became the official state flower. This flower can be found throughout the state. It has long stalks and pale ivory flowers that bloom in early summer. It has broad, sharp leaves that can grow to 2 feet (0.6 m) long. Early pioneers called these flowers "our Lord's candles," because they look like snowy white candles. People have used the roots of the yucca in soaps and in shampoos. The leaves of the yucca can be used to make rope, baskets, and even sandals.

1

Start by drawing a long, thin triangle.

2

Next add some wavy lines for branches.

3

Draw a diamond with a dotted line over the main branch to make the shape of the plant.

4

Using the diamond as a guide, draw little wavy circles for the flowers.

5

Finish the flowers and erase extra lines. You can add triangles for the leaves at the base of the plant.

6

Add as much shading and detail as you'd like.

The Roadrunner

The roadrunner is a bird that would rather run than fly! It is 2 feet (0.6 m) in length and has a long bill and brown feathers. This bird can run from 15 to 20 miles per hour (24–32 km/h). Its official name is the chaparral. Pioneers traveling along the Santa Fe Trail in the late 1800s called it the roadrunner, because they watched the bird run past their wagons. The roadrunner became the official state bird on March 16, 1949. It nests in cactus trees and eats insects, lizards, mice, and snakes. Today it often can be seen running along the highways of New Mexico.

1

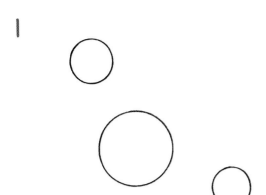

Start by drawing three circles for the rough shape of the roadrunner.

2

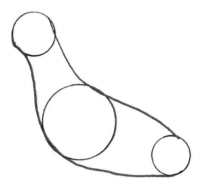

Connect your circles to form the shape of the bird's body.

3

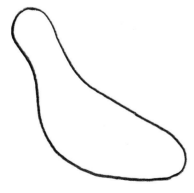

Erase extra lines and smudges.

4

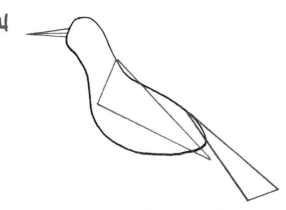

Add a triangle with a line down the center for the beak. Add another triangle for the tail and one for the wing.

5

Erase extra lines. Draw the legs, the feet, and an eye.

6

Add shading and detail to your roadrunner, and you're done. You can also smudge your lines to make the shading more natural.

The Pinyon

The pinyon became New Mexico's state tree on March 16, 1949. This tree grows throughout New Mexico. It is a strong, slow-growing evergreen that only reaches a height of 30 feet (9 m). Tiny nuts, often called pine nuts, grow on this tree. When the cones of the tree open, the nuts fall to the ground. Native Americans used the nuts in many foods, and pine nuts are still popular in cooking today.

Every few years, pinyon trees produce a bumper crop of nuts. When this happens, New Mexicans rush to pick their share of the nuts. During the cold season, people burn pinyon logs in their homes, partly to keep warm and partly because of the wood's pleasant scent.

1

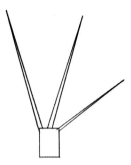

Start by drawing a rectangle. Add three triangles for branches.

2

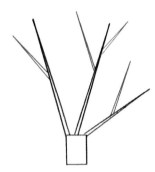

Add four thin triangles for more branches.

3

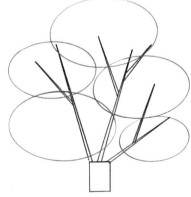

Add five ovals around the branches for the shape of the tree's leaves.

4

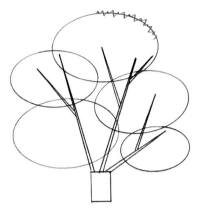

Draw little M shapes around the ovals for the tree's leaf clusters.

5

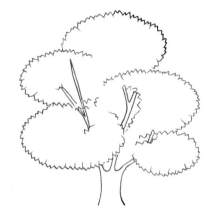

Finish the leaves, and erase extra lines. Let some of the branches show. Smooth the lines of the tree's trunk. Erase extra lines.

6

Add shading and detail to finish the tree.

The Tarantula Hawk Wasp

Schoolchildren chose the tarantula hawk wasp as New Mexico's state insect in 1989. These insects build their nests in the ground. The wasps are black and have dark wings. Sometimes they have blue, orange, red, or white on their bodies. The male's antennae are straight. The females have curved antennae. Tarantula hawk wasps have very long legs and often can be seen running along the ground or resting on low plants. Their sting can paralyze prey a lot bigger than the wasps, including large spiders such as tarantulas. After paralyzing it, the wasp drags the spider to its nest and lays an egg on it. When the wasp egg hatches, the larvae feed on the live tarantula.

Start by drawing a triangle for the wasp's head.

2

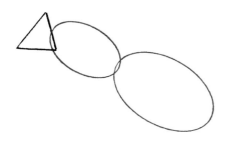

Add two ovals for the outline of the wasp's body.

3

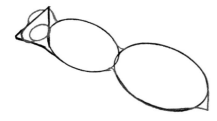

Draw additional shapes and lines for the wasp's head and body as shown.

4

Erase extra lines. Draw two triangles with round bases for the wasp's wings.

5

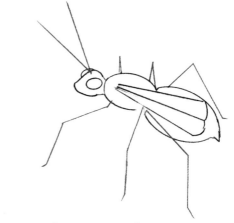

Erase extra lines. Draw the antenna and the legs using both straight and curved lines.

6

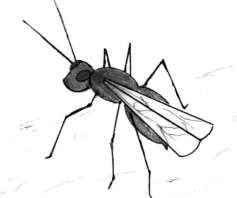

Add shading and detail to your picture, and you're done.

The Coelophysis Dinosaur

On March 17, 1981, the Coelophysis dinosaur was selected as New Mexico's state fossil. In 1947, a scientific expedition found a Coelophysis fossil just north of Santa Fe. Coelophyses were no more than 9 feet (3 m) long. It was discovered that the bones of this dinosaur were hollow. This is why it didn't weigh very much, about 50 pounds (23 kg). This is also why it got its name, because Coelophysis means "hollow form" in Latin. Archaeologists think that this dinosaur ran very fast. Unlike most dinosaurs, the Coelophysis probably ate other animals, including small reptiles, amphibians, and mammals.

1

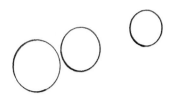

Start by drawing three circles for the dinosaur's body.

2

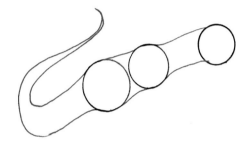

Connect the circles to form the shape of the body. Add a tail.

3

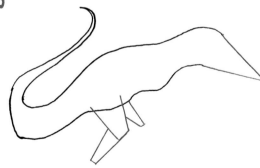

Erase extra lines. Add a triangle for the dinosaur's head. Add shapes for the back legs as shown.

4

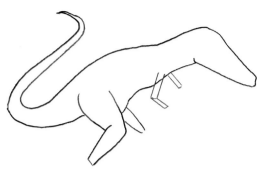

Erase extra lines. Fill in the upper part of the back leg. Add front legs as shown.

5

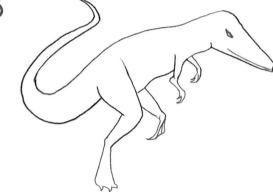

Erase extra lines. Add feet, an eye, and the outline of the dinosaur's mouth.

6

Add shading and detail to your picture.

The Black Bear

In 1950, a black bear was found in New Mexico's Lincoln National Forest. Officials named the bear Hotfoot. At the time, the U.S. Forest Service was using a cartoon bear named Smokey Bear as a symbol for fire prevention. Hotfoot became a real-life image for Smokey Bear.

On February 8, 1963, the black bear was chosen as New Mexico's state mammal. Black bears can live from 15 to 30 years. Female bears can have up to four babies, or cubs, at a time. In 1984, a U.S. postage stamp was designed with a bear cub clinging to a burnt tree. This was the first stamp to honor an individual animal.

1

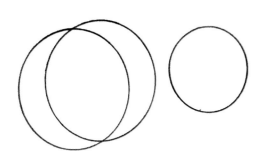

Start by drawing three circles for the bear's head and body.

2

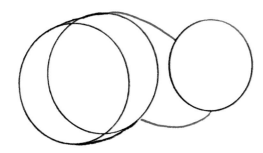

Connect the circles to form the shape of the bear.

3

Add the bear's legs using the shapes shown. Erase extra lines.

4

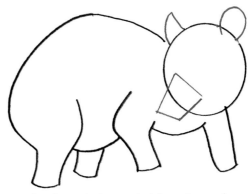

Shape the bear's legs. Add a slanted rectangle for the snout. Add ears on the bear's head. Erase extra lines.

5

Add paws, a nose, and eyes. Erase extra lines.

6

Add shading and detail to your picture, and you're done.

New Mexico's Capitol

New Mexico is home to both the oldest and one of the newest state capitols in the country. This is because the Palace of the Governors, the first capitol building in New Mexico, is still used today. This building was built in 1610. Today this palace is the site of the state history museum. The Roundhouse, the new capitol, was dedicated on December 8, 1966. It has a round design that looks like the Zia sun symbol. Within the walls of this building are artwork and handcrafted furniture made by the people of New Mexico. The building and its contents represent New Mexico's history, from the ancient Native Americans who first lived on the land to today's modern-day society.

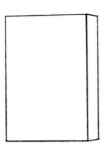

Start by forming two rectangles for the front of the capitol building.

2

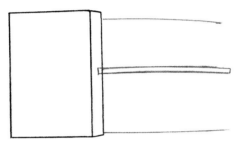

Add two curved lines and a thin, curved rectangle for the right side of the building.

3

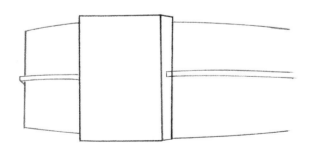

Add two slanted rectangles to the left side of the building. Add another thin, curved rectangle.

4

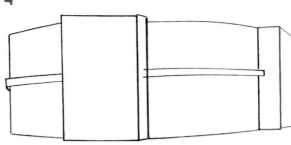

Draw the right side of the building using angled lines as shown.

5

Erase extra lines and add thin rectangles for columns. Add windows and doors.

6

Finish the windows. Add shading and detail. You can also add a clock and a flagpole in front.

New Mexico State Facts

Statehood	January 6, 1912, 47th state
Area	121,593 square miles (314,924 sq. km)
Population	1,739,800
Capital	Santa Fe, population, 62,200
Most Populated City	Albuquerque, population, 448,600
Industries	Agriculture, mining, and tourism
Animal	Black bear
Languages	English and Spanish
Bird	Roadrunner
Flower	Yucca
Song	"O Fair New Mexico"
Fossil	Coelophysis dinosaur
Tree	Pinyon
Gemstone	Turquoise
Insect	Tarantula hawk wasp
Motto	*Crescit eundo*, "It grows as it goes"

Glossary

adobe (uh-DOH-bee) Brick made from dried mud and straw.

amphibians (am-FIH-bee-uhnz) Animals that live both on land and in water.

ancient (AYN-chent) Very old, from a long time ago.

antennae (an-TEH-nee) Thin, rodlike organs used to feel things, located on the heads of certain animals.

architecture (AR-kih-tek-chur) The science, art, or profession of designing buildings.

bumper crop (BUM-per KROP) An unusually large crop that is produced only once in a while.

convert (kun-VURT) To change from one religious belief to another.

dunes (DOONZ) Hills of sand piled up by the wind.

emblem (EM-bluhm) A picture with a motto.

enchantment (en-CHANT-ment) The condition of being very enjoyable or likeable.

evergreen (EH-ver-green) A shrub or tree that has green leaves or needles all year long.

gypsum (JIP-sum) A type of mineral found in the dunes of New Mexico.

larvae (LAR-vee) The plural form of larva. The early life stage of certain animals that differs greatly from the adult stage.

monument (MAHN-yoo-mint) Something built to honor a person or an event.

mythical (MITH-ih-kul) Made up.

paralyze (PA-ruh-lyz) To have lost feeling or movement in the limbs.

prey (PRAY) An animal that is hunted by other animals for food.

reptiles (REP-tylz) Cold-blooded animals that hatch from eggs, such as crocodiles or snakes.

sacred (SAY-kred) Highly respected and considered very important.

talons (TA-lunz) Sharp, curved claws on a bird.

tourism (TUR-ih-zem) A business that deals with people who travel for pleasure.

Index

Web Sites

To learn more about New Mexico, check out this Web site:
www.nmculture.org

J 743.8 WEINTRAUB
Weintraub, Aileen
How to draw New Mexico's sights and
symbols

19 ROSWELL BRANCH

SEP 2 2 2005

DISCARDED
ROSWELL

Atlanta-Fulton Public Library